D0940717

FROGS &
TOADS

First published in Canada by Whitecap Books
351 Lynn Avenue, North Vancouver, British Columbia, V7J 2C4

Text and illustration copyright © Random House Australia Pty
Ltd, 2000

ISBN 1-55285-130-3

Children's Publisher: Linsay Knight
Series Editor: Marie-Louise Taylor
Managing Editor: Marie-Louise Taylor
Art Director: Carolyn Hewitson
Design concept: Stan Lamond
Production Manager: Linda Watchorn

Illustrators: Garry Fleming, pages 1, 3, 8–11, 18–23, 34–47, 50–57;
Dr David Kirshner, pages 4–7, 12–17, 24–33, 48–49,
Consultant: Martyn Robinson, Australian Museum
Writer: Pamela Hook
Educational Consultant: Pamela Hook

Film separation by Pica Colour Separation Overseas Pte Ltd,
Singapore
Printed in Hong Kong by Sing Cheong Printing Co. Ltd

For permission to reproduce any of the illustrations in this book,
please contact Children's Publishing at Random House Australia,
20 Alfred Street, Milsons Point. NSW 2061. fax: 612 9955 3381

When you see a word in **bold** type, you'll find its
meaning in the Glossary at the back of the book.

FROGS & TOADS

Consultant **Martyn Robinson**
Illustrators **Garry Fleming,
Dr David Kirshner**

WHITECAP
B O O K S

CONTENTS

CONTENTS

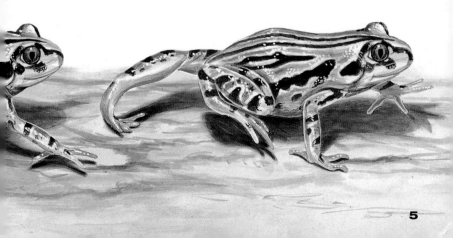

Let's go!

Frogs have been around since the time of the dinosaurs. Today, scientists have discovered about 3,500 species of frogs and toads. They delight us with their brilliant colours, unusual textures, and fascinating behaviours.

AN ADVENTUROUS LIFE

Frogs and toads lead an adventurous life. A 'Pacman' frog is no exception. It begins its life in water as one of thousands of eggs in a mass of jelly-like material. It hatches into a tadpole and spends time feeding and growing in the water, breathing with gills and gradually changing its body shape. Legs replace the tail. Lungs replace the gills, as its new life on land begins. In time, Pacman will find a partner and mate. Another **life cycle** will begin.

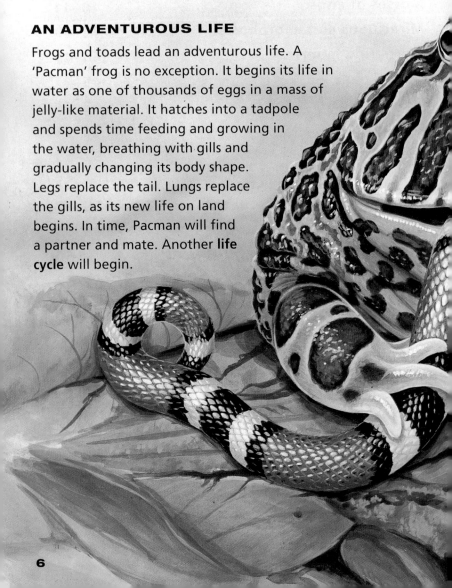

All **species** of frogs are given a scientific name written in Latin or Ancient Greek, languages all scientists understand. The scientific name for Pacman is *Ceratophrys ornata*, which means 'ornate, decorated headpiece'. The headpiece looks like horns but it's really only upper eyelids. The South Americans have given this frog many common names, like the horned toad.

'Pacman' gets its nickname from its enormous mouth (like that of the Pacman computer game character). The mouth enables the frog to tackle large animals, like this coral snake.

This frog bites to defend itself and would give you a nasty nip if you tried to pick it up.

LOOK AGAIN!
The fake horns are used for disguise, helping it to look less like a typical frog.

Amazing amphibians

*Frogs and toads belong to a group of back-boned animals called **amphibians**. They are the best known amphibians but other interesting ones are salamanders, **newts** and caecilians (say-SIL-ee-ans).*

A tiger salamander can replace a leg or tail if one goes missing.

An Asian tree toad is a true toad with dry warty skin. It can climb trees!

A caecilian is a long, burrowing animal with no legs.

Scientists have found frog fossils dating back 190 million years. In fact, amphibians were around before the dinosaurs. All backboned land animals today can trace their ancestry back to early amphibians. Imagine! You have an amphibian way back in your family tree!

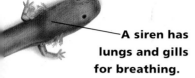

A siren has lungs and gills for breathing.

An Australian red-eyed tree frog has fully webbed hands and feet to help slow its fall from the treetops.

Tomato frogs from Madagascar are very popular as pets because of their beautiful colour.

The horned toad, *Phrynosoma*, is actually a reptile and not an amphibian at all.

MORE ABOUT AMPHIBIANS

'Amphibian' means 'two lives'. Amphibians usually begin life in water but develop into land animals as they become adults. They are cold-blooded, their body temperature changing with the environment. Amphibians don't have fur, feathers or scales. They have smooth, moist skin through which they can breathe. As young, most breathe with **gills** but adults usually have **lungs**.

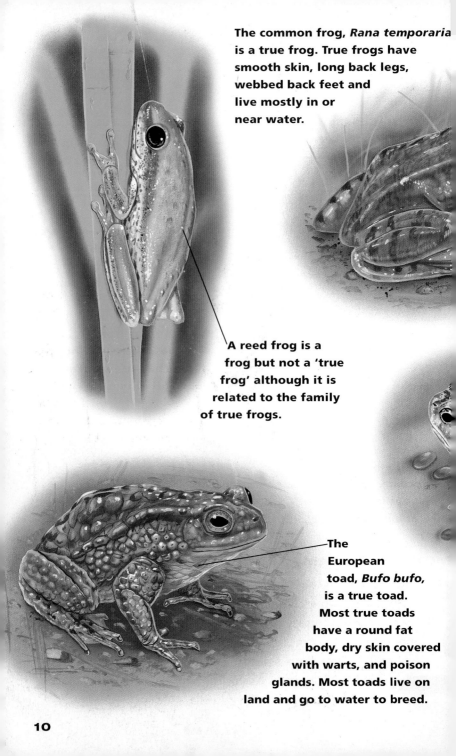

The common frog, *Rana temporaria* is a true frog. True frogs have smooth skin, long back legs, webbed back feet and live mostly in or near water.

A reed frog is a frog but not a 'true frog' although it is related to the family of true frogs.

The European toad, *Bufo bufo*, is a true toad. Most true toads have a round fat body, dry skin covered with warts, and poison glands. Most toads live on land and go to water to breed.

Is it a frog or a toad?

Toads are so closely related to frogs that we could say they are really just another type of frog. There are about 21 families of frogs and toads.

WHAT IS TRUE?

One of the 21 families is called the 'true frogs'. Another family is called the 'true toads'. The rest are quite a mixture because they have some characteristics of true frogs and some characteristics of true toads. Some even steal each others' names and are called toads when they are actually more like true frogs! It's quite complicated even for scientists!

The Australian spadefoot toad is a frog, but they call it a toad!

Toads generally live longer than frogs. The age of one European toad was recorded at 36 years!

t's a frog but some people call it a toad! The Australian crucifix frog, or holy cross toad, gets its name from the cross-shaped pattern on its back.

Skin and bones

*Frogs and toads are vertebrates, animals with backbones. Their skeletons contain a great deal of **cartilage** which makes them very flexible in their movements. Cartilage is like tough elastic. The slimy skin covering the frog's body is also vital to its survival.*

LOOK AGAIN!

The long ankle bones increase the total length of the leg for push off and swimming.

bulbous eye with all-round vision

tympanum or ear drum

short front legs for propping when sitting and cushioning when landing

American bullfrog, *Rana catesbeiana*

webbing between the to for swimming

Frogs and toads generally have a flat head and body, no neck and no tail. As frogs evolved, their back legs became much longer than the front ones and powerful leg muscles developed, enabling them to jump and swim. A frog's skin is thin and permeable, which means it can breathe through it, and absorb water through the skin on the belly. Even in smooth frogs, the skin contains tiny body structures called glands which produce **mucus**, a sort of slime that keeps the body moist. The mucus also protects the animal from **parasites** and **infections**. It also contains a poison which tastes bad enough to discourage predators. Some poison dart frogs produce poison that is so strong it can kill humans. Slime makes frogs harder to hold.

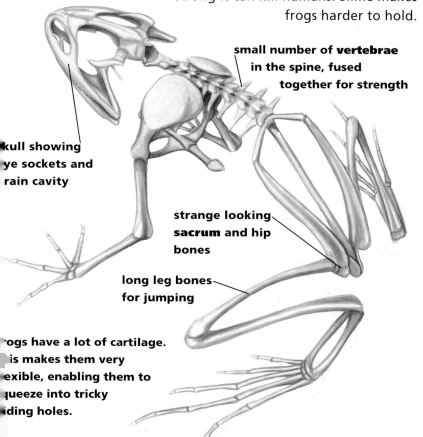

small number of **vertebrae** in the spine, fused together for strength

skull showing eye sockets and brain cavity

strange looking **sacrum** and hip bones

long leg bones for jumping

Frogs have a lot of cartilage. This makes them very flexible, enabling them to squeeze into tricky hiding holes.

The inside story

*Like humans, frogs need to breathe, feed, get rid of wastes, move, grow, reproduce and respond to their environment. Their body contains **organs** and systems that work together to enable the animal to perform all these functions.*

ORGANS AND SYSTEMS

Organs are special body structures that do particular work. The heart pumps blood, the lungs take in oxygen from the air and pass it to the blood, the kidneys filter waste products from the blood, the stomach helps digest food, and the rectum and bladder get rid of wastes. These are just a few of the body organs. Organs work together as a team to form a system. One body system is the digestive system. Its job is to turn food into energy so the animal can perform all the functions needed to live such as breathing, moving and growing.

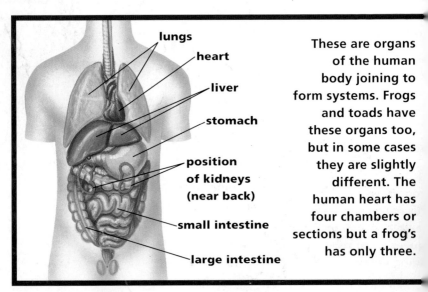

lungs
heart
liver
stomach
position of kidneys (near back)
small intestine
large intestine

These are organs of the human body joining to form systems. Frogs and toads have these organs too, but in some cases they are slightly different. The human heart has four chambers or sections but a frog's has only three.

Here are the organs and systems of a frog. You can see parts of the respiratory or breathing system of the body and also the circulatory system that moves blood through the body. The digestive system is there too. It works to break down food into very simple parts that the body can use. These simple substances are then absorbed or taken into the bloodstream.

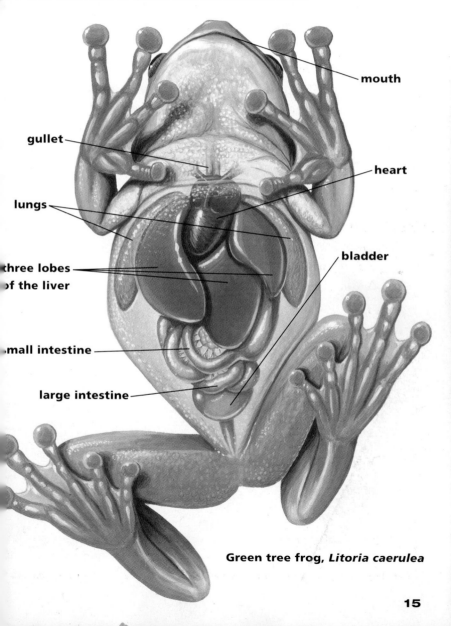

mouth

gullet

heart

lungs

bladder

three lobes of the liver

small intestine

large intestine

Green tree frog, *Litoria caerulea*

Moving about

*Frogs and toads are not just expert hoppers. They can also walk, crawl, swim, glide and dig. Over time they have adapted their body parts to suit their environment and their lifestyle. Webbed feet, toe pads and digging feet are important **adaptations**.*

WAYS AND MEANS

Water-dwelling frogs have webbed feet that work like 'flippers' to push against the water. Gliding tree frogs also have webbing between their fingers and toes and they spread this out to glide and parachute from high rainforest trees. Toe pads act like sticky discs, giving them extra grip to land safely. Tree frogs have sticky toe pads too, which helps them cling to branches.

The Senegal running frog is also a very fast mover. It runs like most other four-legged animals.

It moves one leg and then the oth

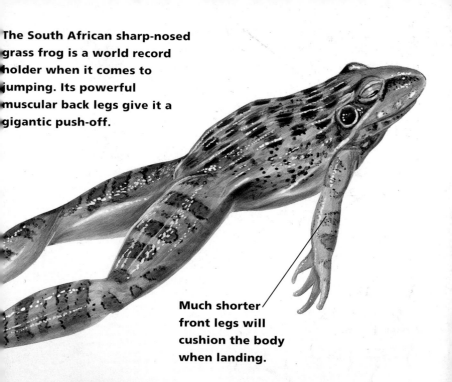

The South African sharp-nosed grass frog is a world record holder when it comes to jumping. Its powerful muscular back legs give it a gigantic push-off.

Much shorter front legs will cushion the body when landing.

LOOK AGAIN!

Frogs and other animals that jump usually have longer back legs than frogs that run.

Some frogs live along streams and waterfalls where they need to hang on to wet boulders.

The right arm moves forward with the left leg and vice versa.

The gliding tree frog from Indonesia has bright green skin for camouflage in its leafy home. The eyes point forward and work like binoculars so the frog can aim for the right landing spot.

Frogs and toads can be found in most unusual places. Some frogs travel about in boxes of bananas being transported to the cities. The green tree frogs of Australia have been known to live in toilets and can even survive the toilet being flushed! Their strong sticky toes help them withstand the current.

The African rain frog copes with dry conditions by burrowing underground. The back feet look like spades and are perfect for digging. Its sandy colour helps the frog blend into the surroundings.

Home sweet home

*Frogs and toads are found on every continent except Antarctica. Their **habitats** range from swamps and rivers to high mountain tops, from dry sandy deserts to steamy rainforests. They are also at home in our cities.*

WHERE FROGS LIVE

Frogs are generally found in or near damp areas. Most need water for egg laying and for the tadpole stage of their life cycle. There are exceptions. Aquatic frogs spend their whole life in water. Where water in creeks and puddles is scarce, certain frogs lay their eggs on land. The tadpole stage is skipped altogether and the eggs hatch directly into frogs.

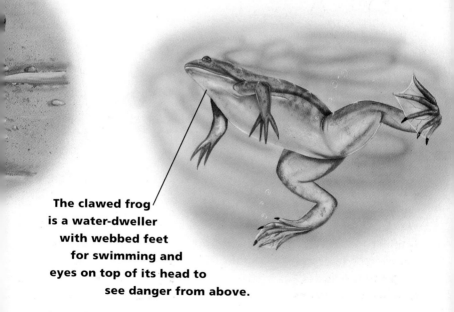

The clawed frog
is a water-dweller
with webbed feet
for swimming and
eyes on top of its head to
see danger from above.

Coping with climate

Some frogs and toads live in areas where intense cold or lack of water is a very big problem. They cope with these extremes in climate by shutting down their systems to save energy.

LOOK AGAIN!

The dry, shrunken water bag tells us that the frog has been there for a while.

The Australian waterholding frog copes with extreme dry by aestivating. It rests in an underground cocoon sometimes for years, waiting for the summer rainfall. The frog relies on stored water and fat in the tissues to keep it alive. Once underground, the frog loosens the outer layer of skin to make a cocoon. Water from its tissues gathers between the cocoon and the next layer of skin. This water bag plus the water still inside the frog, keeps the rest of the frog moist.

The Northern Canadian woodfrog copes with extreme winter cold by hibernating under snow and ice. It finds shelter in a crevice or shuffles beneath the leaf litter under the snow. A special substance in the blood stops the frog from freezing solid. Its cells and vital organs, like the heart and lungs, are protected by large amounts of a type of sugar that can't freeze.

SHUT DOWN

Most frogs and toads prefer warm moist conditions. They are cold blooded so they need to absorb heat from their surroundings. Their skin needs to stay moist to prevent dehydration, the drying out of the body. Frogs cope with extreme cold by hibernating, which means that the body saves energy by shutting down most of its activities and resting in a safe spot. Frogs survive very dry conditions by aestivating. Aestivating is like hibernating but it's done to deal with lack of water. The animal spends the dry season in a state of sleep. Once again, the body shuts down and waits for the drought to break.

Dinner time

*Most adult frogs and toads are **carnivorous**. They feed on other animals. There is a lot of delicious food on their menu—ants, termites, beetles, slugs, snails, earthworms, spiders and even mice and small snakes. Most tadpoles are **herbivorous** (plant eaters).*

FROG FOOD

Frog food varies from a tiny ant to a struggling bat. It depends on the type of frog and the size of its mouth. Food is usually taken alive because it is movement that catches the frog's attention. Frogs rely on their sense of sight. With the slightest suggestion of movement a frog reacts, leaping forward to get closer and flicking out its tongue with the speed of lightning. Some frogs have even been known to eat marbles rolled past them because they thought it was moving prey!

The green and golden bell frog is a cannibal as will sometimes devour one of it own kind. Imagir eating your cousir

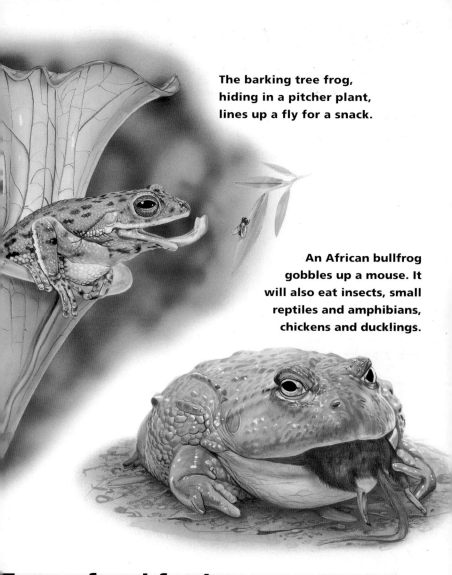

The barking tree frog, hiding in a pitcher plant, lines up a fly for a snack.

An African bullfrog gobbles up a mouse. It will also eat insects, small reptiles and amphibians, chickens and ducklings.

Funny food facts

- Some aquatic frogs take fish that they swallow underwater.
- The Brazilian tree frog is sometimes herbivorous, eating brightly coloured fruit.
- Frogs don't drink water. They absorb it through pores in the skin of their belly.

Tacky tongue

It's certainly not rude for a frog to poke its tongue out because this is the way the animal feeds, with a lightning fast sticky tongue.

Despite popular belief, frogs cannot shoot their tongues out like this lazy European chameleon, a type of lizard.

LOOK AGAIN!

The frog's tongue is short, while the chameleon's tongue is longer than its whole body.

Frog's don't chew their food. They swallow it whole with help from their eyeballs! The eyeballs are pulled back into the skull and they push against the food in the mouth cavity. This pushing action forces the food down the throat.

sticky mucus underneath the tongue

tongue attached at the front

The Australian green tree frog is thought to be the model for Kermit the frog.

If frogs eat something nasty that upsets them, they can vomit it back up again and learn to be more careful next time. Some frogs can even vomit up their stomach, clean off the bad food then put the stomach back!

frog leaping closer to its prey

QUICK AS A FLASH

The frog's tongue is fastened to the front of its mouth and is coated underneath by a sticky substance called mucus. The tongue folds back neatly into the mouth and when the frog wants to feed, it flips the tongue out and the mucus sticks to the prey, rather like hitting a fly with a glue-coated fly swat. The prey is then flicked back into the mouth.

Frog foes

Frogs and toads are tasty treats for a great number of animals, from snakes to spiders and even people!

Humans also eat frogs. Frogs legs are a national dish in France where many native species are disappearing fast.

The cane toad,
Bufo marinus.

LOOK
AGAIN!
The cane toad is trying to protect itself by producing a creamy skin poison.

Snakes are beautifully designed to devour a passing toad or frog because their jaws can open very wide to swallow animals much bigger than themselves. Here we see a South American toad-eater swallowing an inflated toad which has blown itself up either to frighten the snake or to become too large to be swallowed.

Some snakes have special, enlarged 'toad popping' teeth near the back of the mouth. These teeth puncture the puffed-up toad to let the air out, making it easier to swallow.

NASTY PREDATORS

Frogs and toads make a hearty meal for mammals such as raccoons, for reptiles such as snakes, crocodiles and turtles, and for birds like the stork. Frogs also eat frogs. Even spiders can be a real threat if they are big enough to tackle a frog. Fish may sample frog and toad eggs, tadpoles and baby frogs. After all, they share the same habitat. Scientists think that the jelly surrounding the eggs may contain a substance that discourages predators, but even so, fish and newts are known to nibble them. Tadpoles are eaten by a variety of water insects and their young.

Hide and seek

*It is very important for frogs and toads to blend with their environment. They need to stay safe from predators and also to ambush their prey. Looking like part of the surroundings is called **camouflage**. There are lots of tricks to staying alive!*

COME OUT, WHEREVER YOU ARE!

Many frogs spend the daylight hours hiding under rocks and logs, inside crevices in trees or buried in soil or leaf litter. Some hide just as cleverly right out in the open but their camouflage is so good that it is difficult to spot them. Frogs and toads are often the same colour, pattern or texture as the leaves and bark they rest on. Some go further. They have bits and pieces added to their body, structures like horns and pyramid bumps that make the frog look very un-froglike. Even more bizarre are the frogs and toads that mimic unpleasant things—like bird droppings! What animal would choose to eat that?

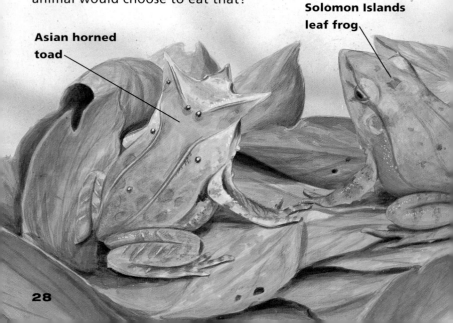

Asian horned toad

Solomon Islands leaf frog

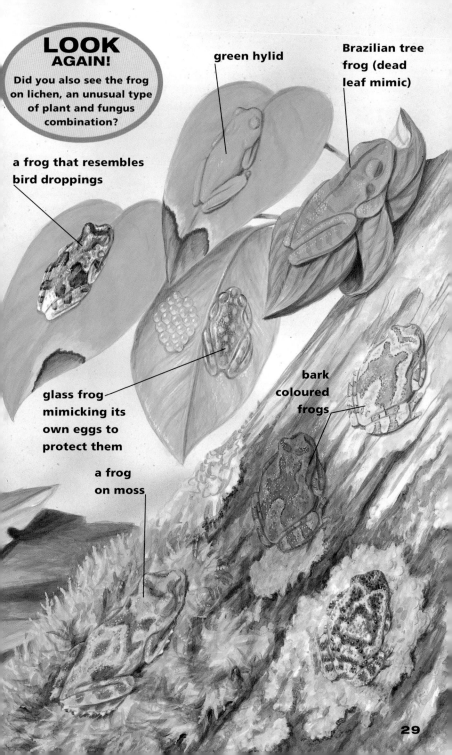

LOOK AGAIN!

Did you also see the frog on lichen, an unusual type of plant and fungus combination?

green hylid

Brazilian tree frog (dead leaf mimic)

a frog that resembles bird droppings

glass frog mimicking its own eggs to protect them

bark coloured frogs

a frog on moss

29

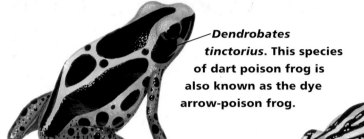

Dendrobates tinctorius. This species of dart poison frog is also known as the dye arrow-poison frog.

The Australian corroboree frog has markings that resemble those used in Aboriginal corroborees or celebrations.

Mantella madagascariensis. As this scientific name suggests, this mantella comes from Madagascar, an island off the east coast of Africa.

A COLOURFUL PARADE

Some frogs are coated with a slimy mucus that contains toxins or poisons, some of which are strong enough to kill animals and even humans. The poison is made in special body parts called glands that may be found under the skin above the eyes, on the thighs or on the back. It depends on the species of frog. To warn predators of their poison, these frogs are often brilliantly coloured in gorgeous reds, greens, blues, oranges and yellows. No hiding for these show offs! They parade their bright bodies instead of hiding away. A predator senses that this colourful animal is dangerous to eat because it is boldly going about its normal business.

Show-offs

Frogs with poisonous skin are often brilliantly coloured to make them stand out, rather than blend in. Some non-poisonous frogs mimic or copy toxic ones, having bright colours as well, just to fool their predators.

This Harlequin frog is actually a toad. Tricky one! Its coloured bands remind us of old-fashioned actors called Harlequins who wore colourful costumes. One species of this frog is thought to be extinct.

The golden mantella is a tiny frog about 3 centimetres (1 inch) long. 'Mantella' seems to be a reference to the word 'mantle' which is a kind of cloak. Mantellas are all poisonous.

Dendrobates lehmanni, a dart poison frog. There is so much variation in the skin patterns of South American dart poison frogs that no two frogs are alike.

The dart poison frogs of Central and South America are so called because the indigenous or native people use the frog's poison to coat the blow darts they use to hunt animals for food. The poison definitely works!

Sudden surprises

Some frogs are full of surprises. They start off camouflaged in their surroundings (page 32) and then, when disturbed by a predator, they put on a most spectacular display (page 33).

FLASHES OF COLOUR

Some frogs have coloured markings hidden beneath the body or legs while the frog is resting. When discovered by a predator, the frog's first instinct is to jump to safety. When it hops, bright colours are revealed. When the frog lands these colours suddenly disappear. This startles and confuses the predator. It is not sure what to do next, giving the frog time to escape. Scientists call these hidden colours 'flash colours' because they appear and disappear.

A. Latin American red-eyed tree frog

B. cane toad

D. *Physalaemus nattereri* from Latin America

C. Oriental fire-bellied toad

At rest, these frogs and toads (page 32) look quite ordinary, but look and see what happens when a predator comes near (page 33).

The fire-bellied toad has underbelly ash colours. If attacked it can flip over its back to show these.

D. *Physalaemus nattereri* does its 'head down, bottom up' act, showing off a couple of huge false eyes to confuse a predator.

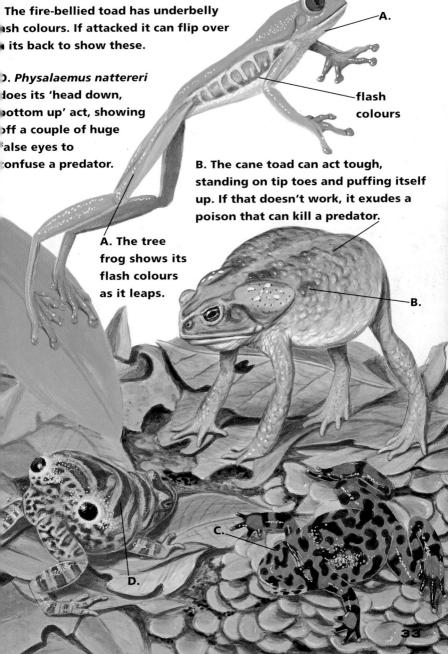

flash colours

B. The cane toad can act tough, standing on tip toes and puffing itself up. If that doesn't work, it exudes a poison that can kill a predator.

A. The tree frog shows its flash colours as it leaps.

A.

B.

C.

D.

Love serenade

At breeding time frogs need to attract a mate. The males serenade the females with love songs that can range in sound from the plunk of a banjo string to the noise of a motorbike.

MAKING A CALL

Frogs breed only with members of their own species and they use special calls to let the right females know they are ready for mating. Frogs and toads have pouches called vocal sacs, formed from the floor of the mouth. Each sac is very elastic, stretching like a balloon and vibrating like the skin of a drum. To make a call the frog fills its lungs with air, closes its nose and mouth and then moves the air over the **vocal chords.** The moving air causes the vocal pouch to vibrate. The vibrating air carries the sound to the outside of the body, rather like the beating of a drum.

Banjo frog ('plonk'). The male frog makes a single 'plonk' call rather like a plucked banjo, hence its name.

ach frog species has its own
pecial sound. However, with
o many frogs calling at
ight it is very difficult to
vork out which frog is
vhich. Some frogs share the time
o that no two males call at the
ame moment. Others call in
horuses, all at the same
me from the same area.
ere are some popular frog
ounds for you to practise.

Common frog, *Rana temporaria*
('grook grook grook'). It has a
vocal sac on each side
of its head.

Striped marsh frog
('tok', like a struck
tennis ball). It can be
heard calling from
suburban fishponds.

Pacific tree frog
('ribbit'). This frog
has the most
famous call of all.
You often hear this
call in movies.

Painted reed frog
(short loud
piercing whistle,
with about two
calls every three
seconds).

Crucifix frog
('whoooop', like an
owl). This frog calls
as it floats. Its vocal
sac makes use of the
whole body, and
ripples in the water
show the effort made
to produce a call.

at barred frog ('wah wah', first
rises in tone, second call falls).

When words fail

As well as calling, some male frogs and toads attract a mate by changing colour during the mating season. They may also have to work hard to protect their breeding site from competing males, so they sometimes go to battle.

Male strawberry dart poison frogs fighting for the best breeding site. These frogs have poison that is used by native Indians to tip the darts of their blow pipes. Unfortunately, the poison doesn't seem to work against rival male frogs!

LOOK AGAIN!

Dart poison frogs get their poison from the ants and millipedes they eat.

Male golden toads, now believed to be extinct, turn a solid gold colour when mating time comes around. The females are also spectacularly coloured with black and red markings.

ON THE BATTLEFIELD

Some male frogs and toads fiercely defend their breeding place. They call to let other males know that the place is occupied. If another male enters the territory, the owner will face the invader and then move towards him, sometimes changing his call to an 'encounter call'. This says, 'Watch out!' A battle may result, with frogs struggling and even biting each other to settle the dispute. Fearsome weapons have been developed to win fights over the best breeding sites. Long teeth, thumb spikes and powerful muscle-packed arms are useful fighting tools for some species. Injuries can be serious and sometimes fatal.

The mating dance

Once a mate is chosen, most frogs find a suitable breeding place, and that usually means in or near water.

FERTILISING THE EGGS

For an egg to develop it must be fertilised. The egg produced by the female must join with the **sperm,** the male reproductive cell. The joining of the egg and the sperm is called **fertilisation**. In most frogs and toads fertilisation occurs outside the female body and in the water. Sperm leave the male through the **cloaca** (klo-AY-kah), an opening at the back end of the body. In order to fertilise the greatest number of eggs, the male places his cloaca as close as possible to the female opening. The male grasps the female and waits until she is ready to lay the eggs. The female pushes out her eggs from her cloaca. As she does so the male spreads his sperm over her eggs and the male and female reproductive cells join. Fertilising the eggs as they emerge is called spawning.

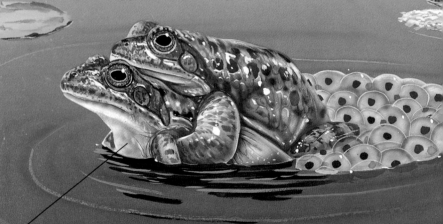

The common frogs spawn in water with the male's arms under the female's armpits. The eggs with their black centres float in a type of protective jelly raft.

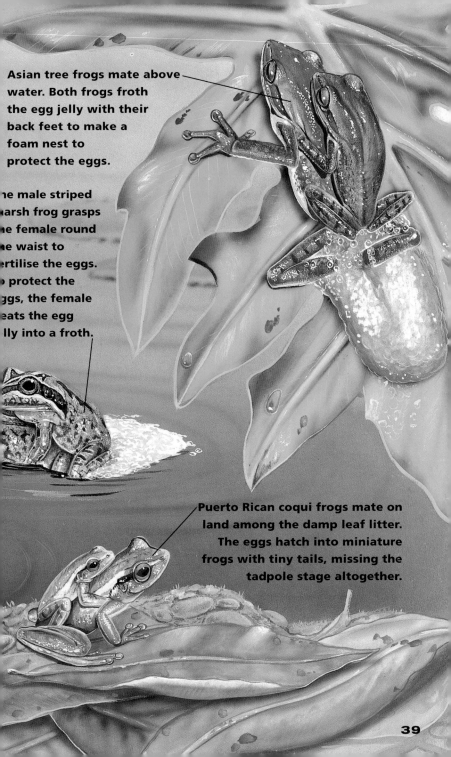

Asian tree frogs mate above water. Both frogs froth the egg jelly with their back feet to make a foam nest to protect the eggs.

he male striped arsh frog grasps ne female round ne waist to rtilise the eggs. protect the ggs, the female eats the egg lly into a froth.

Puerto Rican coqui frogs mate on land among the damp leaf litter. The eggs hatch into miniature frogs with tiny tails, missing the tadpole stage altogether.

The jelly-like material protects the egg from mould and predators, and it can cushion the egg centre from rough water movements. It also helps nourish the **embryo.**

A pair of common frogs add to the already large mass of eggs. Each egg swells and absorbs water as soon as it is laid.

These toad eggs are arranged like a string of pearls in a necklace, and are tangled among the water plants.

Some frogs lay their eggs on the underside of leaves that overhang water. The hatching tadpoles can splash down into the water below.

Masses of eggs

Most frogs lay lots of eggs to ensure that some at least will survive. Eggs can be laid in ponds, streams, water-filled treeholes, on leaves overhanging water, on the ground and in burrows. The list could go on and on!

ALL ABOUT EGGS

Most frogs lay their eggs and forget about them. However, they choose places where the eggs and tadpoles will have a good chance of survival. The eggs are usually laid in water, but many kinds of frogs cope with very challenging habitats where water is not readily available. Some species lay their eggs on land and the tadpoles wriggle or are carried to water! The arrangement of eggs varies as well. The eggs can be laid individually, in small clumps, or in a single large jelly-like mass. Toads tend to lay their eggs in strings.

LOOK AGAIN!

The black colouring of the egg yolks protects them from the harmful rays of the sun.

Miraculous metamorphosis

*Tadpoles change into frogs by using their tail and gills to develop legs and lungs. The changing of an animal from one body form, like a tadpole, to a completely new one, like a frog, is called **metamorphosis.***

EXCEPTIONS TO THE RULE

Most frogs and toads have a life story similar to the common frog but some skip a couple of stages. For example, the eggs of the Puerto Rican coqui hatch straight into baby frogs. Tadpoles differ as well. Most tadpoles eat only plants, but those of the American spadefoot toad are carnivores and cannibals!

1. The life cycle of the common frog is an interesting story that begins as the eggs are laid in the water and are fertilised. The eggs are then left to continue developing.

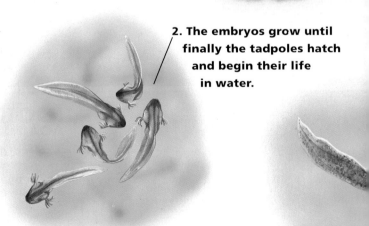

2. The embryos grow until finally the tadpoles hatch and begin their life in water.

6. The tail gradually shortens as it is absorbed until it finally disappears. The young frog leaves its old environment for a new way of life, mostly spent on land. When the adults reach the breeding age, the life cycle starts all over again. There is a picture of a pair of adult common frogs on pages 40-41.

5. Although the back feet show first, the front feet develop at the same time but inside the body. The tadpole pushes them out when they are fully formed.

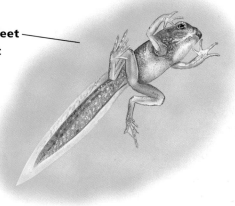

. The tadpole
eeds and grows
n the water.

4. Then the miracle of meta- morphosis takes place. The tadpole begins to change itself into a completely new form. New structures such as the legs and the lungs develop. The gills disappear.

Mothering mums

Most frogs and toads lay their eggs and abandon them. In some species very few eggs are laid so the females ensure that as many as possible will hatch. Let's meet some of these dedicated mothers!

Gastric brooding frog

These were the only animals in the world known to brood their eggs in the stomach! The tadpoles metamorphosed in the stomach and then the mother spat up the tiny frogs. Sadly, both species of brooding frogs are thought to be extinct.

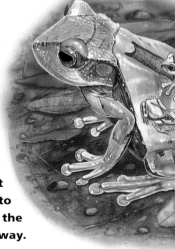

Marsupial frog

The female has a brood or breeding pouch on her back. During mating, as the eggs are laid, the male frog guides the fertilised eggs into the pouch where they are safely carried until hatching. In some marsupial frogs the eggs develop into frogs but in other species the eggs hatch into tadpoles and the mother must sit in the water so they can swim away.

Strawberry dart poison frog

After the eggs are laid and fertilised on land, the mother guards the eggs until the tadpoles hatch. Then she carries the tadpoles, up the trees and places them in water-filled plants called bromeliads, one tadpole per plant. Bromeliads have really tough leaves growing around a central point that fills with water, a neat little tadpole pond. The mother returns and lays unfertilised eggs in the water as tadpole food. Talk about expert mothering!

Surinam toad

These toads swim in a loop formation as they mate. While swimming, the eggs are pushed out and fertilised. As the frogs swim down, the male traps the eggs between his belly and the female's back and pushes the eggs into the spongy tissue found there. Here the eggs continue to develop until they become tiny 'toadlets' and emerge to swim away.

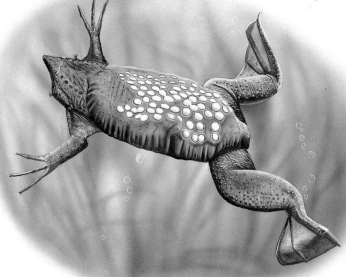

Doting dads

In the frog and toad world the dads sometimes take on the responsibility of caring for the next generation. Here are four very devoted fathers!

Dart poison frog

In the dart poison family the males often help in the transporting of the tiny tadpoles up to the bromeliads in the forest canopy. They do this in the same way the female dart poison frogs do (see pages 44–45).

LOOK AGAIN!

The male hip-pocket frog does a similar job as the female marsupial frog (see page 44).

Midwife toad

The male wraps the string of eggs around his back legs and carries them until they are ready to hatch. Then he finds a pond to sit in so the tadpoles can take to the water. While he is carrying the eggs about he must be careful not to be eaten. Luckily, his poison glands protect him.

Hip-pocket or pouched frog

The male babysits the eggs, laid in the damp leaf litter, until they hatch. The tadpoles then wriggle into pockets on the dad's hips and metamorphose there until they emerge as tiny frogs. These frogs live in places where ponds don't last long enough for the tadpoles to develop. This arrangement overcomes the problem of a lack of watery breeding spots.

Darwin's frog

A male Darwin's frog can truly say he has a frog in his throat! The eggs are laid and fertilised on land and when they hatch into tadpoles the male picks them up, places them in his vocal sac and there they develop (without feeding) into 'froglets'! These still have the remains of their tails when they leave his vocal sac.

Freaky frogs

Every frog and toad species has its own set of special characteristics. However, some are truly amazing in the way they differ from what we expect a frog to look and act like.

DIFFERENT NEEDS

Some frogs and toads are unusual because they need to be different if they are to survive. Over time, they have develop adaptations in the form of body parts and behaviours that allow them to cope with challenges like extreme cold, intense heat or lack of moisture for breeding ponds.

This frog is a digger that burrows headfirst! The female lays eggs underground, not in water, and these hatch into frogs not tadpoles.

Australian turtle frog

Casque-headed fro

It uses its head as a door block off crevices has backed into. Tha a neat way to keep out intruders! The mother carr the young on her back.

LOOK
AGAIN!

Notice the turtle frog's well-developed front legs—all the better for burrowing!

Lake
Titicaca
frog

What a baggy looking creature this is with its very floppy folds of skin! These frogs have no lungs and they breathe through their skin. The more skin they have the better, so they have lots of creases and folds.

Notice the rubbery flap around the edge of the duckbill's head and bill? This helps it to seal off the entrance to its hiding spot in a tree.

Duck-billed tree frog

49

Frog feats

In all families of the animal kingdom there are the high achievers. Some have developed a particular characteristic to such an extent that they have become record breakers.

HIGH ACHIEVERS

Scientists can tell us which frogs and toads hold records for being the biggest, the smallest, the most poisonous and so on. The most toxic frog is *Phyllobates terribilis,* a dart poison frog. It is pictured on page 55. The poison from a single frog can kill many humans. The longest jumper is the South African sharp-nosed grass frog (see pages 16–17). It has huge limbs in frog terms, so no wonder it's such an athlete! Now meet the biggest and the smallest frogs. And these are about twice the actual sizes!

The Goliath frog, *Conraua goliath,* is considered to be the world's largest frog. It lives in Africa and is almost as big as a baby human. One was measured at 35.6 centimetres (14 inches) from its nose to where its tail used to be. Compare that with your school ruler! It weighed 3.1 kilograms (7 pounds).

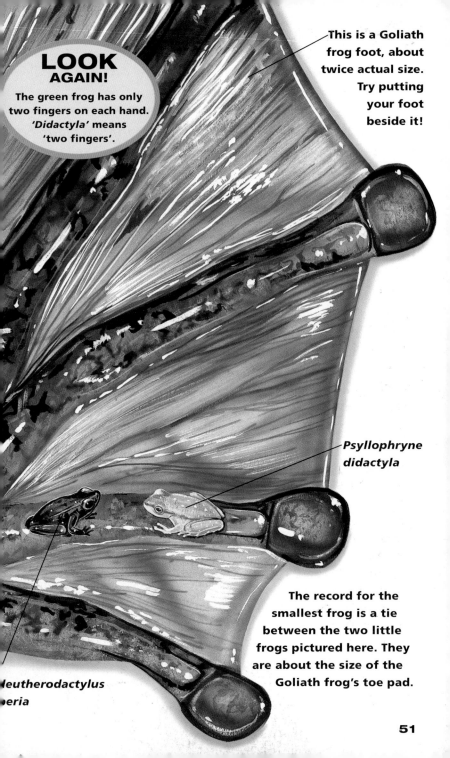

LOOK AGAIN!
The green frog has only two fingers on each hand. *'Didactyla'* means 'two fingers'.

This is a Goliath frog foot, about twice actual size. Try putting your foot beside it!

Psyllophryne didactyla

The record for the smallest frog is a tie between the two little frogs pictured here. They are about the size of the Goliath frog's toe pad.

Eutherodactylus iberia

Farewell frogs!

Frog and toad species have been disappearing at alarming rates since about 1980. It seems likely that humans are interfering with nature so frogs and our planet are suffering We need to take note of the frog's warning.

IMPORTANT CONTRIBUTIONS

Frogs and toads are important because they help to maintain the balance of nature, feeding on and providing food for other animals in the food chain. In particular, they help to keep the insect population under control! Frogs contribute to medical research. The glands of some frogs and toads contain chemicals used to produce medicines such as painkillers and antibiotics. Scientists call some frogs '**indicator** species' because they respond quickly to changes in their environment. When large numbers of frogs disappear, it may mean that the environment is in trouble. We have interfered with nature by draining swamps and ponds, damming rivers, clearing forests and introducing predators. If we lose frogs now it could be a sign of big problems ahead. We need to take action to look after our planet.

Frogs gone

These frogs and toads are thought to be extinct:

- both species of gastric brooding frogs
- Costa Rican golden toads
- Californian red-legged tree frog
- one species of harlequin frog
- the armoured mist frog

The good news is that not all frogs and toads are disappearing. Some species thought to be extinct have been found again so there is still hope. What can we do to protect frogs and toads

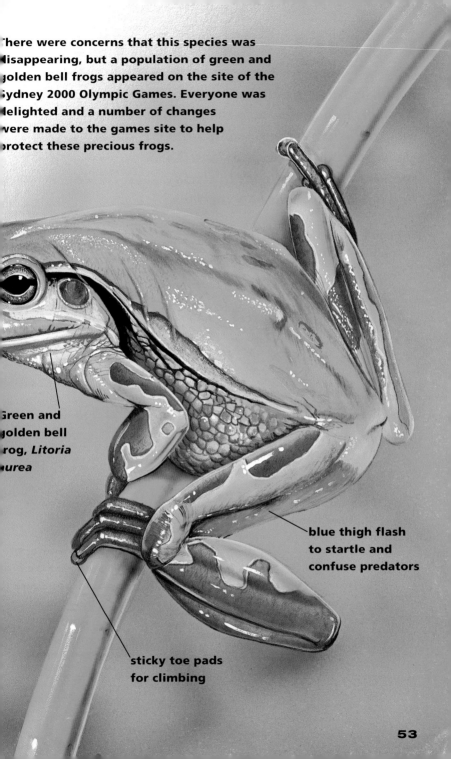

There were concerns that this species was disappearing, but a population of green and golden bell frogs appeared on the site of the Sydney 2000 Olympic Games. Everyone was delighted and a number of changes were made to the games site to help protect these precious frogs.

Green and golden bell frog, *Litoria aurea*

blue thigh flash to startle and confuse predators

sticky toe pads for climbing

Frog families

Scientists study the animal kingdom by organising all members into groups according to their common characteristics. Organising into groups is called **classification.** *There are at least 3,435 species of frogs and toads to classify. Let's find out a little about how it's done.*

European toad, *Bufo bufo*
(Bufonidae family)

Paradoxical frog,
Pseudis paradoxis
(Pseudidae family)

There are 335 different
species of this toad. The
genus and species name
for this frog are the same
and this is unusual.
'Bufo' means 'toad'.

Surinam 'toad'.
Pipa carvalhoi
(Pipidae family)

Another member of
this genus is *Pipa pipa*.
See how frogs share the
same genus but have
different
species
names.

Australian red-eyed tree frog, *Litoria chloris* (Hylidae family)

Sometimes the common name tells us where one species of red-eyed tree frog is found.

The first scientific name (the genus) is like the surname and the second one (the species) is like a first name. There are only three other species in this small family.

Dart poison frog, *Phyllobates terribilis* (Dendrobatidae family)

Ornate horned toad, *Ceratophrys ornata* (Leptodactylidae family)

The scientific name means 'terrible or dreadful leaf frog'. This is the most toxic frog in the world!

This frog is the same species as the Pacman frog you met on pages 6–7. See that the colours and markings are different on each frog. This happens a lot with frogs.

FAMILIES, GENERA AND SPECIES

Frogs and toads belong to a group of amphibians called Anura (An-YOU-rah). In this group there are 21 **families** of frogs and toads. Families are sorted into smaller groups called **genera**. Then these are sorted again into groups where all the members have exactly the same characteristics. This group is called the **species**. Phew! What a job! Most animals are also given an easier name, called a **common name**. On this page are pictures of one member (a species) of six families of frogs and toads.

Keeping a Goliath in your shower

Keeping a Goliath frog in your shower would be such a cool thing to do—for a while! You could end up with no pocket money after helping to pay the water bills!

A FUSSY GUEST!

In the wild, Goliath frogs hang out around waterfalls so the shower would be perfect. But the water would run *all* the time! Your family might choose to go dirty rather than share the cold shower with your froggy friend. The air conditioner would have to be going constantly. They like it cool! Let's hope everyone else does too! And what about food for your special guest? You'd have to catch *lots* of dragonflies and other insects. If your new friend is *really* hungry it might be persuaded to eat some live mice! Now, catching mice could be a challenge. Better talk to the family cat but remember, for a Goliath frog, the only good mouse is a live one! Perhaps it would be simpler to settle for a pond in the garden.

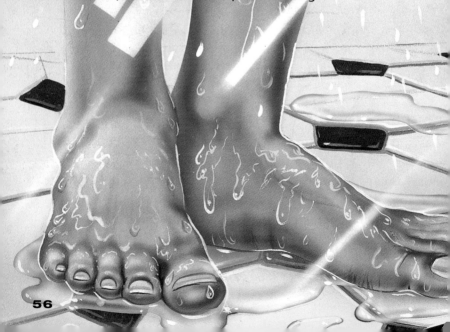

Make your own frog pond

Here are some helpful hints about making a frog home:

1. Have suitable plants in and around your pond. Frogs are happy if they have somewhere leafy to live and hide. The plants will attract food. A few logs and rocks would be appreciated too.

2. Vary the depth of the water as different species like different depths.

3. Build the pond away from bedroom windows. Frogs are committed evening singers and could disturb the family.

4. Keep notes on your frogs.

5. You might be providing a home for a rare species. You and your froggy friends might be famous one day.

GLOSSARY

adaptation A feature of an animal or plant that allows it to survive in its environment.

amphibian (am-FIB-ee-an) A cold-blooded animal with moist skin and no scales, that begins life in the water and lives on land as an adult.

camouflage Colours, patterns or body shape helping an animal blend with its surroundings.

carnivorous Meat eating.

cartilage (CART-ill-aj) A flexible substance that forms part of a skeleton.

classification Arranging animals or plants into groups according to their common characteristics.

cloaca (klo-AY-kah) A single body opening through which the digestive, urinary and reproductive products are passed.

common name A name given to animals and plants in the local language or in popular use. This name is often easier to remember than the scientific name and perhaps tells us something about the animal or plant. For example, *Ceratophrys ornata* has several common names such as ornate horned toad, Pacman frog, horse killer.

ear drum A thin skin in the middle ear that vibrates when sound waves strike it. In frogs and toads this is called a **tympanum,** and is visible behind the eye.

embryo (EM-bree-oh) A developing animal, waiting to be born or hatched.

fertilisation (FER-till-I-ZAY-shun) The joining of a male and female reproductive cell to form a cell that will develop into a new individual.

fossil The remains, imprint or other sign of an animal, plant or other feature from ancient times that has been preserved in rock.

fungus Any one of a group of plant-like organisms without leaves, flowers or chlorophyll.

genera (JEN-er-uh) More than one group of related animals or plants. *See* **genus**

genus (JEE-nus) A group of related animals or plants having certain body parts or functions in common that make them more closely related to each other than to other groups. Scientists give an animal two scientific names: the first name for the genus group, a bit like a surname; and the second name for the **species,** like a first name. For example, *Ceratophrys* (genus) *ornata* (species). That is, there are several species with the genus name *Ceratophrys,* but only one of those is *Ceratophrys ornata.*

GLOSSARY

gills Body parts that absorb oxygen from the water, allowing tadpoles to breathe.

glands A body organ that makes substances to form a secretion useful to the body, such as a toad's poison.

habitat The place where an animal lives.

herbivorous Plant eating.

indicator A species of animal or plant whose presence or absence in an area tells us about special environmental conditions.

infection Disease that can often be spread from one animal to another.

life cycle The development of a living thing from the beginning of its life until it becomes an adult and reproduces.

lungs Breathing organs of the body that take in oxygen from the air, pass it to the bloodstream and remove carbon dioxide from the body.

metamorphosis (met-ah-MORE-foe-sis) A marked change in body form and habit of an animal during its development after the early hatching stage to when it becomes an adult, such as from a caterpillar to a butterfly.

mucus (MEW-kus) A slimy substance produced by the body.

newt A small salamander that lives part of the time in water.

organ Any part of a plant or animal where the tissues are organised to do a special job, for example, heart, lungs.

parasite An animal or plant that lives and feeds on another animal or plant without killing it.

sacrum (SAY-crm) A bone at the lower end of the spine forming the back of the pelvis.

spawn (SPORN) A mass of eggs produced by fish and other water creatures, or the act of producing these.

species (SPEE-sees) The individual kinds of plants and animals. *See also* **genus**.

sperm One of the cells of the male that fertilises the eggs of the female.

tympanum (TIM-pan-m) *See* **ear drum**.

vertebrae (VER-t-BRAY) Spool-shaped bones that join together to form the backbone. For one we say vertebra.

warts Small, firm lumps on the skin.

FIND OUT MORE ABOUT FROGS & TOADS

BOOKS

Clarke, Barry, *Amphibian,* Dorling Kindersley, London, 1993

Mattison, Chris, *Frogs & Toads of the World,* Cassell plc, London, 1998.

Cogger, H. G., and Zweifel, R. G., *Reptiles and Amphibians,* UNSW Press, Sydney, 1998.

WEBSITES

http://www.exploratorium.edu/index.html

The Froggy Page
http://frog.simplenet.com/froggy

The Somewhat Amusing World of Frogs
http://www.csu.edu.au/faculty/commerce/account/
frogs/frog.htm

United States Fish & Wildlife Service—Kids Corner
http://endangered.fws.gov/kid_cor/htm

Yahoo! Pets
http://pets.yahoo.com/pets/noah_s_ark/
reptiles_and_amphibians/

INDEX

NDEX

FREE

 INVESTIGATE

POSTER!

Collect 6 of the gold  INVESTIGATE stickers

(you will find one on the stickers' page in each book)

**Send all 6 stickers on a sheet of paper
along with your name and address to:**

Investigate Series Poster
Whitecap Books
351 Lynn Avenue
North Vancouver
British Columbia
V7J 2C4

and we'll send you your free INVESTIGATE **series poster**

Please allow 21 days for delivery.